CHRISTIE DAWN

MERRY ME!

A Funtastic Guide To Help You Embrace Your Inner Child & Live More Joyfully

Joy [joi]

Colourful bubbles rising up from the heart,
filling the body and causing one's face to
light up!

With a sunny smile and sparkly eyes, I feel
like a child, full of wonder and awe!

What does joy look like to you?
Would you like to experience more of it in
your life?
What brings you joy?
How often do you do that which brings you
joy?

Contents

Preface

I've written this book because I feel like the world could use more joy. A *lot* more. Much of the focus in today's world, at least through many media streams, is on the yucky stuff. The doom and gloom. Or just the less desirable stuff we don't want to see, hear or think about. And it's pretty in our faces, isn't it? I'm not saying we should ignore important issues, but rather we shift our perspective and give more attention to the good stuff; focus on positive solutions rather than the problems; invite and allow more joy into our own lives, and in turn be able to share more with others. After all, what we feed grows!

I believe *everyone* deserves to experience (more) joy, and I want to help people do that. I think everyone has room for more of it in their life. And the more joy we experience, the more we experience joy! There is magic all around us if we just open our minds, hearts and eyes! Play is essential to our well-being at any age, not just in childhood. We all need a bit of silliness in our life! My hope is for people to be happy.

My goal is to help people live more joyfully and have more fun. I wish to inspire and help people discover, or re-discover, what brings them joy so they can do more of it. I wish to help people (re)connect with their inner child and experience the wonder of life! The world can seem like such an ugly place sometimes, and it's up to us to live a life of joy. We are responsible for our own happiness and when we realize that, we take back our power and can make life as great and magical as we desire!

Introduction

Sure, life can be challenging. No one said it would be easy. But it can be joyous and fun and magical too! And the power is yours to make it so.

Did you know some of the most common regrets people have expressed in their last days were that they didn't live a life true to themselves or allow themselves to be happier? [1] How sad is that? Especially since it's so preventable. I don't know about you, but I do not want to be left with regret when I reach the end of my time here on Earth. I want to be able to say I lived a life of joy; a life that I loved; a life that inspired others.

It all starts with believing you are worthy and tweaking your mind-set/beliefs/conditioning. Small, manageable (but mighty!) changes in your perception, routine, etc. Little changes that will have a big impact. I know, I know, the scary "C" word. But these changes aren't scary. They are just itty bitty. Until you feed them and they grow bigger! <insert best roar here>

Ponder this for a moment- if stress can have such a negative effect on our health, (and I assure you it does), just imagine how living more

---

[1] Reference from 'The Top Five Regrets Of The Dying' by Bronnie Ware, published by Hay House Inc. August 2019

joyfully can impact our well-being. If we all started living more joyfully, what a grand shift the world would make!

So, who wants to rediscover that child-like wonder? That lust for life? And start living a life that brings you more joy? Seems like a no-brainer to me. And you've already taken the first step by picking up this book. Congratulations! Now let's get livin'!

I am not a doctor, I only aim to inspire.
I want to make it clear that my intention with this book is not to "fix" anything, because nothing is "broken". Nor am I implying that we must feel joy all the time and disregard the less desirable emotions. That would be unrealistic and absurd. There is room for all emotions in our life and all are valid. Of course, you don't need me to tell you that. I just want to be clear about my intentions with this book, which is to help you live *more* joyfully and experience *more* moments of joy in your life, IF that is what you desire.

This book is intended to provide real results through inspiring individual exploration in regards to what makes *you* happy. Because what makes me happy might not bring you the same joy. So while I do provide examples based on my own experiences and what I've learned, which will hopefully inspire you as well, this is really about finding what works for you by encouraging you and prompting your own self-exploration/discovery of what lights you up so you can do more of it. It's about giving you an opportunity to explore/journal/make notes about *your* discoveries so you have something to go back to later when you need some inspiration. Essentially, so you can inspire yourself and not have to rely on others to do so!

So here's to the journey of discovering and living a more joy-filled life! A world of possibilities await you!

Maybe you'll find you're already doing many of these things. Great! Keep it up! And please let your abundance of joy spill out into the world and inspire others. But for those of us that truly desire more out of life- more fun, more magic, more of what feeds your heart and soul and lights you up, this book is for you!

How To Use This Book

In my own personal experience, overwhelm suffocates any chance of progress. So I need to be very mindful that I take small, manageable steps to ensure I keep moving forward. And I need to make it **FUN**!

I've designed this book in such a way that you can take little nibbles, only as much as you can absorb at one time. That being said, I recommend first reading it straight through, beginning to end, at your own leisure of course, then going back and working through it however feels right. Just let whatever jumps out guide you. Flip through, and whatever grabs your attention, dive in!

Use this book as a guide, a reference, a companion to living more joyfully. Come back to it as often as you need/want. Make notes about your own findings and what works for you. Pick one new thing to implement into your life, one thing that really lights you up. Master it! Then pick another. And another. Repeat, repeat, repeat. Until your life is so full of joy that you can't help but let it spill out into the world and affect all those around you! I wish you fun, magic, happiness, and an abundance of JOY on your journey! Here's to joyful living! Here's to YOU!

Welcome Joy Seekers/Farewell Fun-Suckers

Halt fun-suckers and destroyers of joy!

By the wave of my magical wand I command you to freeze in your tracks! Make the decision right now to drop this book and:

-Go back to settling for good/okay/fine/comfortable/the usual

-Only looking forward to the weekend, summer or whatever to let loose a little for a limited amount of time before returning to the daily grind/your regularly scheduled program/ordinary humdrum life

-Rinse and repeat until you die, and just before you die, lament and regret all the things you didn't do and now it's too late

OR, get ready to set flight to *EVERLAND*! Where anything and everything is possible! Where people *DO* like Mondays! And Wednesdays are wonderful! And Fridays are just like any other day, only because every day is awesome! Now don't get me wrong, there is a time and place for seriousness, but most of us take life (and ourselves!) far too seriously far too much of the time. And life is too short for that.

So come away with me on a real life adventure that never ends, and finally create an amazing life that you don't need to escape from! If you've got the guts that is. C'mon, I triple dog dare ya!

(After that introduction, you're probably expecting that you'll need to make massive changes in your life to be able to live this new exciting life, and in a way you're right. But massive change comes from taking many small steps. So fear not, tiny human! You can do this! *Anyone* can! Alright then, let's get livin'!)

The idea of living more joyfully may sound delightful to some, but unattainable to others. *How* to live more joyfully might seem obvious to one person, but foreign to the next. But despite that, I truly believe that every single person is completely *capable* and *deserving* of experiencing joy. And it starts with *allowing* ourselves to.

One

Here I Am, I Am Here (Being Present)

Can't wait for the weekend to finally have some fun? Why wait?! Have fun NOW! Quit waiting for circumstances to change to live a life you actually enjoy living! How can you truly experience joy if you are not fully present in the moment?

Let's say you are out in the woods having a picnic with your family, but every two minutes you are on your phone, responding to messages or whatever. There is very little that is so urgent it needs your immediate attention and can't wait for an hour or two. We live in such a fast-paced world where we've become accustomed to expecting everything immediately. But we really need to learn to slow down a bit. How can we ever enjoy or appreciate anything when our mind is always somewhere else? Not being present makes it pretty much impossible. So here's my challenge to you: practice ditching distractions and allow yourself to be fully present in the moment. Allow yourself to really experience and appreciate where you are right at this moment. It might feel weird at first, but this is our true nature.

Try leaving your phone at home (or at least put it on silent) when you go for a walk and just notice all the beauty around you. Look at the trees, the sky, the people. Appreciate it all. Breathe deep. Allow yourself to just feel and appreciate everything around you without being distracted. Wherever you are, whoever you're with, practice being present, without distractions. That alone can make a world of difference in your life!

Allow yourself to enjoy things NOW! Use the fancy dishes! Wear the fun clothes! Quit reserving everything for a special occasion! Today *is* the special occasion! The very fact that you are alive and part of this world is cause to celebrate! Right now, today, this moment, is all we're promised. Actually, we aren't even promised that. So LIVE! Like you mean it! Live with passion and JOY!

Drink water from a wine glass! Slurp chocolate milk from a Donald Duck cup! Heck, wear a Donald Duck costume if you feel like it! If Elton John can do it, why not you? Because you're not a rock star? Yeah you are! You ARE a rock star! The rock star of your life, so go out and live it!

What are some things you can do to practice being more present in your life? Use the free space that follows to brainstorm/dream/draw/etc.

Two

What Goes In, Must Come Out!

~Be mindful of the fuel you feed yourself~

You know that old saying "garbage in, garbage out"? What we feed not just our body, but our mind and our spirit really has a big impact on the quality of our life. Everything we take in affects our reality: the food we eat, the movies we watch, the music we listen to, the books we read, and most importantly, the stories we tell ourselves, the words we use about ourselves and the world around us.

What does your inner dialogue sound like? How do you talk to yourself and about yourself? How do you talk about life in general? Do you use loving, life supporting language? Or sabotaging, negative talk? Start to take note of this. But be gentle with yourself! If you notice yourself fueling up with energy that doesn't serve you well, instead of scolding yourself, *celebrate* the fact you caught yourself! And then see if you can come up with a more supportive alternative. The more you do this, the easier it becomes to make choices based on what brings you joy and makes you feel good, alive and healthy!

An example for me is scary movies. I do not enjoy them. They do not put me in a good frame of mind and they do not make me feel good. So why on earth would I want to watch them?! Why would I intentionally feed myself something that causes me to feel bad and does not bring me joy? I wouldn't! So I don't. Simple. Now, this is a really easy one. Or so it seems. So start with ones that are simple and obvious to you and work up to the more challenging ones.

An example of a more difficult one might be indulging in foods that we *enjoy,* but don't make us feel very good after eating them. Maybe we have an intolerance to that particular food, or maybe it's just not a healthy choice. So we do experience joy, but it's short lived and replaced with any number of not so pleasurable experiences. Stomach ache, headache, whatever. So here lies the challenge. We need to weigh out the good and bad individually and choose ultimately what is best for us. Find our own personal balance and try to avoid stepping over that fine line between pleasure and pain. Just play around with it until you find what works best for you. Again, go easy on yourself. Just begin to be aware of how things make you feel. Are you feeding yourself life-supporting energy, or life-sucking energy?

*Important note: I am in no way offering dietary/nutritional advice. I am only encouraging you to be mindful of what you feed yourself and how it ultimately makes you feel. Whether it be food, thoughts, words or whatever. Rather than mindlessly ingesting what maybe doesn't serve you well.

Action steps:

- Start to notice the language you use/how you talk about yourself and life in general. Is it kind/helpful/true? Does it nurture or hinder your happiness? Is it life supporting or life destroying? Start by just becoming aware, and then move on to changing that dialogue to a more loving one.
- Notice what kind of TV shows, movies and music you choose. How do they ultimately make you feel? Do they make you feel good? If not, maybe start questioning why you choose what doesn't make you feel good, and challenge yourself to start choosing what does.
- Pay attention to the types of people you spend time with. Do they lift you up, or bring you down? They say we become like the people we spend the most time with, so choose wisely!
- Look at your surroundings. Your home, decor, clothing. Does it reflect who you are and who you want to be? Are you a bright and colourful person always dressing in black? Or an eccentric circle living in a grey, square house? Think about new ways your environment can support a more joyful life for you.

Notes:

Three

Be a Waterfall of Gratitude!

~Fill your heart with gratitude. Practice being grateful every day~

It's not always easy to feel grateful, especially when things seem to be going badly. And we all have days like that. You know the kind. Those days where it's just one thing after another, like a domino effect. You're running late and can't find your keys, then you get stuck in traffic, arrive at work late, etc. And this usually sets the stage for the rest of your day, doesn't it?

Wouldn't it be nice to just stop the "chain of bad luck" in it's tracks and turn it into a "wave of good luck"? Are you aware that you actually *can*? If just one seemingly bad thing can seem to spawn so many others, why the heck wouldn't the opposite be possible? It IS, silly! And the first step to switching things around is by simply being grateful! And there is *always* something to be grateful for. Always.

Start looking for things to appreciate, big or small. A flower, a conversation with a loved one, a smile from a stranger. The sun, the moon, the stars. A warm bed to sleep in, food to eat. Start with just one thing and include it in your daily routine. It could even be giving thanks for simply waking up each morning. Life itself is indeed a gift to be grateful for. It might not always feel that way, especially when times are rough, but the more you practice gratitude, the more you'll find you have to be grateful for!

Start small. Just one thing each day. Until it becomes a natural part of your day. Then add another. And another. Make each thing as big or small as you like, but mean it. Now, I know this can be much more of a challenge while experiencing difficult times, so start practicing now. Practice being grateful when it's easy to do so. And work up from there. Then, when you do find yourself in a sticky situation, it will be so much easier to do so you can quickly break the chain before it actually becomes one.

What are you grateful for?

Start making a list of everything you are grateful for. Make a gratitude folder on your desktop or phone, or even on paper and tape it to your wall. Include photos, songs, videos, whatever takes you to moments you are grateful for. Make a gratitude poster or vision board. Come up with your own ideas to keep yourself inspired to be grateful. Get creative! Have fun with it! Make some notes, draw pictures, or whatever you like below:

Four

Come Out & Play!

That child-like spirit lives on in us forever, sometimes we just bore it to sleep!
Let's shake it awake!

Oooo, this is my favourite chapter! (Aside from the next one, that is.)

Time to reconnect with your inner child! Rediscover that child-like wonder! Play! Imagine! Make-believe!

As adults, many of us have forgotten how to live joyfully, as we did as children. Or maybe we're just discovering now how to live joyfully. For me, I feel I'm experiencing more and more joy the older I get (I must be getting wiser!).

I always tell people I'm much more of a kid now than when I actually was one!

As we "grow up", we are taught or conditioned to get serious about… well, everything! Our careers, our relationships, our finances, our health, etc. We get so obsessed with getting all of these areas of our life "right" that we experience less and less joy, and more and more stress, worry, and even resentment. But all of these areas of life should actually bring us joy!

This idea that fun and play is just for kids…what a hot steaming pile of stinky garbage! I mean really, what a rip off to have to leave the wonder and magic of life behind as we "grow up". Seriously?! We're supposed to just stuff our imaginations into a box at some point and stick it in the attic to gather dust? To heck with that!

Can you imagine telling your younger self this was the way things would be once we began to "grow up"? Man, we'd all have taken off straightaway for Never Never Land NEVER to return! And rightfully so! We are not meant to shelf our imagination or our playfulness or that child-like sense of wonder. And we don't have to. These are essential elements in living a happy life. Life should be fun! It's meant to be enjoyed! Not just as a child, at every age! Your imagination only goes away if you let it. And you only get old if you believe yourself to be!

Think back to when you were a kid. What was your favourite thing to play? What made time stand still? What did you love to do that you got so immersed in that hours passed but it only seemed like seconds? Now, when was the last time you did that? Do you still do it? Why did you stop? Because grown-ups don't play? Because it's silly? Baloney! Who made that ridiculous rule that play is only for children? Well it's not! It's for everyone. And it's actually essential to our well-being.

Now that being said, one of the best and easiest ways to learn how to play again and to experience more joy in our life is to spend time with the pros- children! They are experts at living joyfully! They experience pure joy without even trying.

One of my most memorable experiences with this was sitting at the table with my 5 year old granddaughter and my two nephews, aged two and five. They were enjoying some hot chocolate after a little winter excursion outside, and their chocolate moustaches made me giggle. I was suddenly reminded of that sound that kids often make after guzzling a lot of beverage all at once. You know the one:

"Gulp, ahhhhh!"

I made the sound and it quickly became a game. "1, 2, 3, 4, gulp, ahhhh!" Laughter erupted. Again "1, 2, 3, 4, gulp, ahhhh!" The laughter seemed to grow bigger and louder with each repetition. That pure and innocent laughter was delightful and contagious. That hysterical, deep from the belly kind. One silly little noise turned into a game which resulted in a moment of pure and simple joy. I wish I could have captured it in a bottle to open anytime anyone needed a lift.

And in a way I did. Because now that sound is associated with that moment. All I have to do is make that noise and it triggers that memory and brings me joy. Powerful stuff huh? And the best part is, we can create moments like this anytime we want! But if you need to brush up on your play game, and witness and experience more joy, spend more time with children. Let us learn from the masters!

Playtime prompts:

- Play in the mud/sand/grass
- Roll down a hill
- Puddle-jump
- Blow bubbles
- Colour/paint/sculpt/doodle/draw
- Dress up
- Build a blanket fort
- Make believe
- Let your imagination run wild!

Add your own ideas here:

Playtime props:

- Crazy sunglasses
- Colourful clothes & accessories
- Kooky costumes
- Clown noses
- Bike horns
- Whoopie cushions
- Kazoos
- Silly Putty
- Playdough
- Kinetic sand
- Lego

Write more of your own below:

~A bit of silliness is good for the soul~

Don't be afraid to let out your quirky kookiness! Let your freak flag fly high in the sky, straight on till morning!

Silliness prompts:

- Make funny faces
- Walk a funny walk
- Talk a funny talk

Your own space to play:

Five

A Dose of Magic!

How dreadful would a world without magic be? I just can't even imagine! And I don't mean pulling rabbits out of hats (although that kind of magic is fun too). I mean the kind of magic that surrounds us every day! The kind we're usually too busy to notice. You know, like life itself! Do you ever just stop and think about how *magical* the very fact that we are alive and breathing and doing all these things every day is? Well, you should! It's a good place to start! From there, you can amp up the bonus magic! There are a million (at least!) little things you can do to make life more magical. It will look different for everyone, of course. But I'll share some prompts to get the wheels spinning. Read on for ideas and make notes about how you can make your own life more magical!

Extraordinary Alterations

Take something ordinary and make it extraordinary! Something you use all the time that you can alter easily enough so that it makes you smile and brings you more joy every time you see/use it.

19

My rainbow painted fan

A friend's trailer I helped paint. (Still a work in progress.)

Brainstorm more ideas!

More things that make life more magical:

- Art
- Music
- Peace
- Love
- Dance breaks
- Fairy lights
- Star gazing
- Blanket forts

- Rainbow window cling
- Prisms
- Magic globes
- Imagination
- Appreciation
- Gratitude
- Playfulness
- Colour

Make the ordinary extraordinary!

How can you make your life more magical? What are some things you can do?

Here's another idea to make mundane tasks more joyful: make your to-do list more appealing! Draw bubbles or flowers or hearts on a blank page and write each task into each shape. Wrap your chores in love and playfulness! Make the bubbles multi-coloured or brush a kaleidoscope over a bouquet of flowers! Do whatever to make that dreaded list visually more attractive! From there, work on making each task more fun to do with music or whatever. And be sure to add a few "tasks" that actually do bring you joy! Sneak in some dance breaks, walks, etc.

Bonus tip: Add the more enjoyable things into the bigger bubbles (or hearts, etc.) and the less fun things into the smaller ones. A little trick to make the bigger tasks look smaller and more manageable! Don't forget to check each one off as you complete it. (Especially gratifying for us list makers and tickers!) Add more as you go if you get everything done and feel you'd like to accomplish a bit more. They can be all fun, rewarding things if the must-do's are out of the way. The feeling of achievement, big or small, feels joyful!

Make your own fun to-do list below!

Six

Listen To The Music

You're in line at the grocery store, the waiting room at the doctor's office, or any other number of not so exciting scenarios. Suddenly a song you haven't heard for years comes on: one you totally forgot about, one that you used to really love. Hearing it again fills you with immense joy. You're so grateful to be hearing it again and can't believe you forgot about such a great song! And just like that- a rather mundane situation becomes an absolute joy! It makes you forget where you even are!

I am a huge fan of music. I can't even fathom *not* loving it! Like *whaaat?!* If you happen to be someone that doesn't, I strongly urge you to give it another chance. Listen to little bits of all different kinds until you find something you like. Music is such a beautiful, magical, powerful thing. It can change your mood in an instant. It can take you back to a precise moment in time, or make you think of a particular person. It can transport you to another world! And it can bring *SO* much joy! It can really work wonders I tell ya!

I've had the extreme pleasure of witnessing the true power of music in so many instances in my life, but I'd have to say the most amazing has been seeing it appear to dissolve dis-ease, particularly of the brain.

My grampa lived with Alzheimer's for a number of years before he passed away. Near the end of his life, I and a musician friend went up to visit him. He appeared quite vacant by this point, staring blankly much of the time. My friend started playing guitar. He played some of my grampa's favourite old songs. And I swear you could see the light just switch on in his brain. I'm certain he remembered these songs and how much he loved them. It's the most incredible thing to see the power of music on the brain. I learned that my grampa used to play guitar himself and would try serenading my grama, lol. My friend put the guitar in my grampa's lap and he gently started strumming the strings. I'll never forget that.

*There's a lot of information linking the positive effects of music on brain-related diseases and disorders (you can find out more on the Alzheimer's Association's website among others).

~Music can have a profound effect on our mind, heart and soul~

If you're new to the wonderful world of music and need a kick start, I've included a list of some of my favourite feel good tunes on the following page(s).

And for my fellow music lovers…

What's your favourite song? What song lifts you up? Inspires you? Empowers you? Put it on! Turn it up! Dance to it! C'mon, like you mean it!

Expand on this by creating a whole playlist. Title it JOY or HAPPY or whatever resonates with you. Listen anytime you need or want a lift. Make more playlists. This is one of my favourite things to do because I love music, and there is such power in music. It can alter your mood in a split second. So make it good! It's a super simple, fun (and physical) way to instantly change your mood and lift you into a higher energy frequency/vibration. Feel free to start your list below!

As promised, for the newbies, here are but a few of my favourites that put me in a good mood without fail!

   *(live vids are best! Just type in the search on You Tube) I dare ya not to dance!

- Happy Days Toy Town by The Small Faces
- Sing, Sing, Sing by Benny Goodman
- I'm Shakin' by Jack White (original written by Rudy Toombs, first recorded and released by Little Willie John)
- Your Auntie Grizelda by The Monkees
- Shake a Tail Feather by Ray Charles & The Blues Brothers
- Only The Good Die Young by Billy Joel
- Better Move It On Home by Dolly Parton & Porter Wagoner
- Sunshine Daydream by The Grateful Dead
- Boogie Shoes by KC & the Sunshine Band
- All Together Now by The Beatles
- Home (and pretty much anything else) by Edward Sharpe & The Magnetic Zeros
- Red Palace by Spider John Koerner & Willie Murphy
- Tiger Feet by Mud
- Groove Is In The Heart by Deee-Lite
- Mama Weer All Crazy Now by Slade
- Surrender by Cheap Trick
- The Beat Goes On by Sonny & Cher
- Little Bitty Pretty One by Thurston Harris
- Vacation Time by Evan Johns and The H-Bombs
- Twistin' the Night away by Sam Cooke (I also like the Rod Stewart version)
- Toast of the Town by Motley Crue
- Good Vibrations by The Beach Boys
- Whole Lotta Lovin' by Fats Domino

- I Love To Boogie by Marc Bolan (type in "Marc Show I Love To Boogie" in You Tube)
- Soul Man by The Blues Brothers (original by Sam & Dave) *bonus dose of happy that signature Blues Brothers dance!

Woo! Just had me a little dance break myself there! Good fun and a good little reset! *(See next chapter for more on dance breaks!)

*I also strongly suggest you check out your own local music scene. Go to live shows, buy albums and merchandise. Support your local musicians!

Seven

Let's Get Moving!

You ever get in that space where you just feel stuck? Maybe you're stuck in your brain and that leads to actually feeling physically stuck? I have. Many times. And in my experience, not much feels less joyful than being stuck or stagnant. The longer I am inactive, the less energy I seem to have, and the worse I feel, physically and mentally. So please, don't forget to move!

No matter how busy you are, no matter your level of ability, keep moving in whatever way you can. It makes a huge difference in how you feel (and think). As always, make it fun! Choose movements that make you feel good! Maybe it's yoga. Maybe it's running. Maybe it's dancing or roller skating or skipping rope. There are a gazillion possibilities! Play around with it and find what feels good for you! Again, I'll share some prompts below for inspiration.

Movement prompts:

- Dance breaks (Make playlists of your favourite songs, set an alarm for specific times throughout the day where you drop everything and dance, even for just 5 minutes.)
- Go on a mini hike (or a big one!). Get out and explore nature, or even your own neighbourhood
- Go for a bike ride
- Climb a tree (but be careful!)
- Get up and stretch! (Especially if you're sitting for extended periods of time.)
- Go bowling
- Go swimming
- Go for a jog
- Take dance lessons
- Do yoga
- Take up kick-boxing
- Learn to ride a unicycle
- Practice juggling
- Try Tai Chi
- Play on the monkey bars
- Dooo you playyy…crOHHH-quet?!
- Anyone for tennis?
- Shake it off! (Stand up, or sit down if standing is not manageable, and literally shake your body off, like you're trying to get something yucky off of you or like a wet dog does to get dry.)

*Again, please only do what your body is capable of doing safely.

Write some of your own ideas about how you can move joyfully here!

Eight

Adjust Your Lens (Perspective)

~If you change the way you look at things, the things you look at
change~
~Dr. Wayne Dyer

Attitude and frame of mind have much to do with everything. We see
living proof of it every day if we open our eyes and look. So: what will
you choose to focus on?

If I had a bag of pixie dust for every time I've heard people talk about
how much things suck, or how they can't wait for the weekend or until
things get better, or this or that, I could fly myself to the moon and back.
"My job sucks", this sucks, that sucks, everything sucks. You know what
sucks? Your freaking attitude, that's what! Sheesh!

But I know how easy it can be to get sucked into that negative drama.
It happens without realizing it sometimes.

But guess what? Life doesn't have to suck.

Yes, life can be hard and can throw us a lot of curve balls. But our frame of mind does play a big role. And tweaking your lens can make a world of difference in how you deal with things.

We can take the seemingly sucky situations and grow them into massive horrible monstrosities, or we can flip that sucker on it's head and make a gosh darn rainbow milkshake out of it, k?

Like, if you think everything sucks, it will. Simple. So every time you find yourself saying or even thinking something sucks, flip it! Find something good about it. (Try harder!) If you really honestly cannot think of anything good, even something so minuscule it barely stays in your brain for two seconds (write it down!), then find something entirely different and separate from the sucky thing that *ROCKS*! Yeah! And focus on *THAT*! And if you really can't find something that rocks, first of all, I call BS, but in that pretty much non-existent case, MAKE something! Make it up! Let your imagination run wild!

Challenge:

Anytime you catch yourself focusing on what you *don't* want, adjust your lens and zoom in on what you *do* want!

Example- "I wish I didn't have to work here. I hate my job."
   <adjust lens>
   "I would really love to have a job doing _____!"

Or,

"I hope I don't catch that flu going around!"

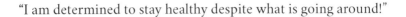

"I am determined to stay healthy despite what is going around!"

Or, change

"This situation sucks."
  to
  "It would be so much better if _____!"

I think deep down, every one of us *wants* to feel joy. It's our natural state. But I think we've been so conditioned to believe that life has to be hard or even miserable. And there are SO many miserable, unhappy people in the world. Why? Is it because of lack itself, or lack of appreciation for what we do have? I believe the latter. And there is proof of it all over the world. It's why someone who appears to have nothing still manages to be happy, while someone appearing to have it all can be miserable.

*Bonus perspective playtime prompt and mood changer: Take up kazooing! Every time you feel anger bubbling up, first acknowledge it, then give it some happy company! Grab that trusty kazoo and blow yell into it with all your might. "I'M SO MAAAAAAAD!!" Repeat as necessary. I'm almost positive it will tame those fiery grouchies!

*Note: you can likely pick up a cheap little kazoo for a few bucks from your local (that's LOCAL) music or toy store.

Or, make one with a comb and a bit of wax paper. Remember making those when you were a kid? Remember how much fun you had?

Ideas:

Nine

Be One With The Sun, Croon With The Moon, Run Wild, Sweet Flower Child!

One of the absolute best ways to experience more joy is to get out into nature. Just *be* with it. *Enjoy* it. *Nurture* it. *Respect* it. *Play* with it. *Learn* from it.

Whether you choose to believe it or not, or as hippie-dippy as you think it sounds, we are all one, all connected- us, the earth, the cosmos, *everything.* So let's start acting like it and start (or continue) to treat all of it (ourselves included) like the beautiful, wonderful miracles we are: with respect, appreciation and love. If we all treat the earth and all it's inhabitants in this way, the reward will be immeasurable.

Get out there! Go hug a tree! They give us clean air to breathe, man! That's a pretty big deal and well deserving of a measly hug, I'd say!

Sit in the woods and observe all the life that's around you. Be still and watch. Birds, butterflies, frogs, snakes, mice, deer, squirrels, rabbits- all of it! Let yourself be in awe of it all! Learn to identify native plants and birds.

Splash in the puddles after it rains. Dance beneath the stars. Blow kisses in the wind. Gaze at the moon. Study the night sky. Get excited as your garden grows. Do anything and everything you can think of to enjoy and appreciate nature!

Have some fun melding the topics covered in this book together. Let imagination in to play while out exploring nature. It's great exercise for the mind.

When I go for a walk in the woods, I see so much more than just trees (not that trees aren't already magnificent all on their own of course!). I see a whole magical world! And it breaks my heart when others can't. Or won't. I think it comes down to being willing. And they might not be because maybe they think it's silly or stupid. I've even seen this with some children. How sad is that?! It seems childhood gets shorter and shorter all the time.

Okay, back to trees. Like I said, they are just spectacular all on their own. But when fantastical creatures emerge from them, it's like you're in a whole other world! It's like your very own fantasy or story except it's real, because it's right in front of you! Even omitting the visions of your own imagination and bringing them to life in the real world, there is SO much wonder in the natural world that goes unnoticed: the details in a patch of moss, the intricate designs on the underside of a mushroom. All because we're always too busy focusing on the destination rather than the journey. Adult brain says "Get from point A to point B. Don't get distracted from the mission." Psh! How boring! Forget that.

Go, get lost! Wander! Explore! The journey IS the destination! So enjoy it! Stop. Breathe it in. Notice how you feel in the moment. Really appreciate the beauty around you. Take pictures if you like. Now, this is pretty easy if you're already in a beautiful setting, but the next challenge will be to start seeing beauty where it may not be so obvious. This can undoubtedly be more difficult, but once you really begin to appreciate it in naturally beautiful settings, it gets easier to see beauty everywhere.

And remember, if you change the way you look at things, the things you look at change! -Dr. Wayne Dyer

And eventually, you'll see the whole world for the magnificent, magical place that it is!

~We can discover the wonders of nature~
-The Grateful Dead

Get out in nature prompts:

- Forest bathing
- Bird watching
- Hug a tree
- Go hiking
- Rock/tree climbing
- Nature photography
- Explore the woods
- Go camping
- Make friends with a butterfly
- Wade in the water
- Just sit and observe!

One with the trees!

Magical sunset over the lake

Making friends with a butterfly!

Communing with the chickadees!

Play with the elements!

Earth

- Build castles/dig/bury yourself in the sand
- Dig in the dirt

Water

- Swim/play in the water

Air

- Blow bubbles in the wind
- Fly a kite

Fire

- Have a bonfire

Blowing bubbles in the wind

Beautiful bonfire to end the day

Explore more ideas of how you can enjoy nature in the wide open space below:

Ten

Simple Pleasures

~Enjoy the little things in life!~

Stop and smell the gosh darn roses!

We're always so busy, rushing here, rushing there, doing this and that and twenty-five other things that we don't often just let ourselves be present and appreciate where we are. We're always rushing to the next moment.

Just stop for a moment. Look up at the sky. Get lost in it's vastness. Get your head *in* the clouds! Hug a tree. Smell a flower. Enjoy the warmth of the sun on your face, or the aroma of your favourite hot beverage. Appreciate the warmth of the mug on your hands. Just stop and appreciate all the things we often take for granted. The more we can appreciate it all and be grateful, the more we'll find to appreciate and be grateful for.

I often get very excited about seemingly small things and people often look at me like I'm a bit kooky. Well, okay, to be fair I am a bit kooky. And I like it that way. But that's not the point. The point is I easily find joy in the simple things in life. And I am very grateful for that. Not everyone has such an easy time of it. But I believe simply allowing yourself to find joy is most of the battle. As I mentioned before, I think many of us feel unworthy of experiencing joy, especially when there is so much pain in the world.

But listen to me when I say this, and listen hard: EVERYONE IS WORTHY OF EXPERIENCING JOY! Got that? EVERYONE. No matter your circumstances or how much money you make or how undeserving you may believe you are. Don't you forget it! So start allowing yourself to experience it.

Start right now. Pick something in the room you are in. Anything. Look at it. Appreciate it for what it is. Appreciate it for what it provides, or how it makes your life easier. Find anything and everything you can about it to appreciate. Feeling joy at this point will just come naturally.

Simple Pleasure Prompts:

- Take your favourite mug. Fill it with your favourite beverage. Look at it. Feel it in your hands. What is it about that mug that you love? Let yourself really appreciate it. What is it about the contents of the mug that you love? Sip it slowly. Savour it. This might seem small and feel silly, but every single thing, big or small, deserves our appreciation and gratitude. So let yourself be fully immersed in it. Appreciating big things is easy. Finding pleasure in the little things we often take for granted- now that's a gift!

Write more of your own ideas below:

Eleven

Let That Joy Out! Be Bold! Be Free! Be YOU!

Alright, it's time to throw all nonsensical rules out the window. You know, those ones that were made up for no good reason. The ones likely made up just to keep the squares and prudes that made them up comfortable. Ones like "You can't wear that; you're too old" or "Pink hair is for teenage girls" or any other nonsense that's ever kept you from expressing yourself freely and joyfully.

The only rule here is don't hurt anybody. You want pink hair? Have pink hair! You want to wear a rainbow tutu? Wear a rainbow tutu! Dress how you feel and feel how you dress. Wear clothes that make you feel good and happy and alive! Want purple walls and a blue ceiling and painted murals instead of carpeting? Do it! Decorate your world with what makes you smile. You want to join the circus? Join the freaking circus! Do things that make your heart and soul sing! Do YOU! Do what brings you JOY! If it is truly bringing you joy and genuinely not causing actual harm to anyone in any way, odds are, it's actually going to bring others joy just by witnessing the joy emanating from you! Happiness and joy are contagious! So let's all start spreading the good stuff around!

Prompts:

- What's your favourite colour? Wear it more! Decorate your space with it. Eat more of that colour (naturally is best, of course). My favourite colour is rainbow- the more colours the better! When I dress or surround myself with lots of colours, I feel happier/better/more alive/full of joy. And it's contagious too! When I dress colourfully, other people comment how bright and colourful I am, how they love it and it brings them joy.

Free to be you space!

Twelve

Shine Your Light!

Be the sunshine in someone's cloudy day! Be the rainbow amidst someone's storm! Spread joy out into the world however you know how, and as often as you can.

The world needs your love light! So turn it on, and LEAVE it on!

Start doing more of what you love and then share it. The world needs your unique brand of joy! What good are the gifts we were given if we keep them hidden?!

I know how scary it can be at first, trust me. I have struggled with shyness and self-confidence my whole life. But the more you do something, the more comfortable you get. And when you witness the joy it brings others, well that's the ultimate motivation to keep going!

Just start with one small thing and go from there. Maybe it's just simply smiling at strangers as you pass by. Maybe this would be huge for you because you are so shy that the thought of even looking at someone in the eye frightens you. Challenge yourself to smile at just one person. But I must warn you, smiles are contagious much of the time; odds are, whoever you smile at will smile back! On the flip side, some people are just determined grumpy pantses and will dig their feet into the gunky swamp of despair no matter how much it hurts. Smile harder. I betcha you can crack them eventually!

For you more daring souls, choose something bigger! Something you've always wanted to do and the very thought of it makes you smile, but you've never quite got enough courage up to do it. Maybe it's sharing your art with the world, performing a song or doing back flips down the sidewalk (please only attempt that last one if you really know what you're doing!). Or maybe you have this crazy desire to dress up as a bunch of grapes, knock on people's doors and tell them you love them (I think this would be great and I would love if this actually happened to me!). Get creative. Have fun! Go spread your joy around, the world needs it!

Write down some crazy fun ideas of how to spread your unique brand of joy below!

Thirteen

Lucky 13 Bonus Inspiration!

Here's a little icing on the cake for you: some people, movies, songs (actually, I already shared some of those in the chapter about music), and more that have been an inspiration to me in regards to living more joyfully. I hope you'll check them out and be as inspired as I have been, and I hope they bring even more joy to your world!

Favourite feel-good/fun movies:

- Patch Adams - Not only an incredibly inspiring movie, but an absolutely outstanding human being, whom you can find and follow on social media.
- Mr. Magorium's Wonder Emporium - It's about a toy store run by Dustin Hoffman (Mr. Magorium) who is the embodiment of joy; I need not say more!
- Unicorn Store - Unicorns, glitter, wonderment and Samuel L. Jackson- c'mon!

- Finding Neverland - If you like the story of Peter Pan, how could you not love the story of how it was brought to life by playful genius novelist and playwright J.M. Barrie?

I have so many favourites so I will stop there and let you write some of your own!

Totally Awesome People That Exude Joy

The following people are so full of life that joy just pours out of them and into the world. You can't help but catch their spirit! At least that's been my experience. I've never met any of them in person, but all of them have inspired me greatly to live more joyfully, more freely, and have encouraged me to be true to myself, whether they know it or not. I'm quite confident you will find their love, passion & delightful quirkiness most infectious!

- **SARK** - Bestselling author, artist, speaker, mentor and a wonderfully fun and magical being that has been such an inspiration to me and so many others.
- **Patch Adams** - Doctor, clown, peace activist and outstanding human being that makes me want to be a better human being.
- **Katwise** - Makes crazy colourful coats and sweaters and lives in a rainbow house and has a painted bus! The first time I stumbled across this magical creature on the internet, I said "This girl is living my dream life!!!" Except that our art forms vary.
- **The Merry Pranksters (past and present)** - Ken Kesey, Neal Cassady, Wavy Gravy, Ken Babbs, The Grateful Dead, a bus called Furthur…I could easily go down a rainbow tie dyed rabbit hole talking about this merry band of beings! Do yourself a favour and learn all about it. So much fun and camaraderie! There are plenty of books, documentaries, etc., and I highly encourage you to seek them out. The most recent one that lit a big ol' let's get livin' firecracker under my butt was a documentary called Going Furthur. Learn more at goingfurthur.com.

Who inspires you to live more joyfully and let your kooky, quirky, wonderful spirit shine?

Favourite Classic Stories/Books:

- Alice in Wonderland
- Peter Pan

Of course there are many, many more, but these are my two absolute favourites. And there are so many versions and reincarnations in writing and on screen. One I saw recently was sort of a take on the two combined. It's called Come Away and you can watch it on Netflix.

What are some of your favourite stories that inspire you to live more joyfully?

Fourteen

Conclusion

Go Forth, Joyful Spirit! Be Free! (Taking Action and Making It Real!)

There is this saying, "If it's important, you'll find a way; if it's not, you'll find an excuse." If you constantly find yourself making excuses, is it because you feel obligated to do things that don't bring you joy and that you don't really want to do? Or is it because you feel undeserving of that which does bring you joy? Start asking yourself this question and see what you find.

If you're anything like me, you get easily overwhelmed. You get super excited and ambitious and want to do/try everything all at once, but this creates overwhelm and ultimately inaction. So you end up doing very little, or nothing at all. And then you end up disappointed.

This is precisely why I offer suggestions and ideas that are small, manageable and can be easily applied. I strongly suggest implementing them in small increments. One small step at a time. One new idea at a time. So it becomes a lifestyle and a natural part of your life, and not just an experiment.

I think we underestimate the power of taking tiny steps forward. We tend to believe we need to make big, drastic changes all at once. But again, that's when overwhelm sets in and ultimately leads to inaction. So it's far better (and less stressful!) to focus on one small, simple step at a time and consistently move forward towards bigger goals. Remember, slow and steady wins the race! (Although this isn't a race.)

We want to create lasting change here. And it should be *fun*! It's intended to be fun! Not a chore. You're much more likely to stick to something if it's fun. And this is what this is all about, right? Creating more joy! *Experiencing* more joy! So if it's not fun and enjoyable, what the heck is the point?! Okay, so after a week or two focusing on one new, fun habit…once you are confident this has now become a regular, natural part of your life, time to add the next one!

So, we've covered quite a lot here, and I know how overwhelming taking in a lot of information can be and then actually applying it. I do it all the time - get real excited and enthusiastic about something and want to do everything all at once.

Please do not attempt to apply all of the ideas in this book at once. In my experience, and I'm pretty certain it's this way for everyone, overwhelm ultimately leads to inaction. I want to prevent that from happening. Please take one little step at a time. Pick any one suggestion and work on it until you nail it. Until it becomes a natural part of life and you don't even have to think about it. It just happens. You just do it. It's automatic. And then add another. And another. There is no particular order here. Work through it in any way you want. Start in the middle if you like and work outwards. Jump around from chapter to chapter if you want. Go back and re-read as much as you need to. Make your own notes and refer back whenever inspiration is needed.

But start by simply asking yourself in everything you do- does this bring me joy? If yes, great! Keep doing it! If not, ask yourself if it's something you really have to do. If not, ditch it! If so, ask yourself how you can make it more enjoyable (by the way, there's *always* a way!).

Tips: play music you love while doing it, smile while doing it, be grateful that you are *able* to do it, and reward yourself for getting it done!

Just really begin to recognize what brings you joy. Recognize the feeling of joy. *Allow* yourself to feel joy. And get used to it, because you're about to experience a lot more of it! So long as you commit to yourself to do what it takes to make it happen.

And once you get real good at experiencing joy yourself, share it! Because what's better than doing that which brings you joy, than sharing it with others. It amplifies the joy. So once you find what brings *you* joy, share it!

What brings me immense joy, is creating joyful experiences to share with others. I love throwing theme parties and just fun events in general. Halloween is a big one for me. I am the self-proclaimed Queen of Halloween. Some people find this strange as I do not enjoy scary movies and such, as I mentioned before, but for some reason I do love Halloween!

Of course, any day is a good day for a party! When my kids were little I would spend so much time creating decorations and props for their birthday parties. One of the most fun ones I threw was for my eldest daughter. It was a carnival themed party. I used big cardboard boxes and painted them up to create a popcorn stand, some kind of clown toss game and other fun stuff. I'm not sure who had more fun, the kids or me!

Another time I got inspired watching the movie Patch Adams and just had to try to re-create the balloon scene, which the real Patch did in real life many times I believe. So for my youngest daughter's 15th birthday, I attempted to fill the entire living room with balloons to surprise her (I haven't done this since as I'm always at least trying to be more environmentally conscious). But I have to say, it did create a neat memory and a fair bit of joy!

I just love creating moments like this. If I could just do that, every day, that would be pretty freaking fantabulous!

Here's a space I'm creating for you to fill with what lifts *you* up! Write your ideas in the eco-friendly balloons below!

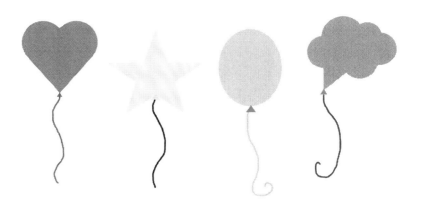

If you can manage to take even one idea offered in this book, and apply it to your life to create more joy, then you've achieved success in living more joyfully. Anything else is icing on the cake.

If you'd like to get in touch with Christie, you can email her at christie@rainbowearthcreations.com. To learn more about her colourful creations & experiences, visit rainbowearthcreations.com.

Many thanks to Chelsea, John, Megan, Nadine, Katherine, Sharon, Paula and George for their feedback and support. And thank you to my wee fairy hippie mama for her patience, love and support always.

Manufactured by Amazon.ca
Bolton, ON